D1221592

The purpose of this study guide is to provide supplemental educational material. It is not intended as a substitute or replacement of DRACULA.

Published by SuperSummary, www.supersummary.com

ISBN – 9798504964287

For more information or to learn about our complete library of study guides, please visit http://www.supersummary.com

Please submit any comments, corrections, or questions to:
http://www.supersummary.com/support/

TABLE OF CONTENTS

Dracula is a gothic novel by Bram Stoker published in 1897. Stoker tells the story of the fight against the vampire Dracula in an epistolary format. The story comprises various letters, telegrams, journal entries, and newspaper articles written by the main characters. *Dracula* explores the classic theme of good versus evil, but the novel also illuminates the relationships between religion and reason, the East and the West, the modern age versus the old world, and how the repressive mores of the Victorian era clashed with more liberated ideas about female. The novel's influence on Gothic, horror, and romance genres was profound, and the character of Count Dracula became one of the most influential, recognizable figures in literature, film, television, and even video games.

Plot Summary

Dracula is set during an unnamed year in the last decade of the 19th century. The action begins with an English solicitor named Jonathan Harker traveling to help Count Dracula with legal matters concerning his immigration to London. Dracula is gracious and charming, but also unsettling. Jonathan never sees him eat, he has pointed ears and teeth, and he always ends their conversations just before sunrise. Jonathan eventually learns that he is trapped in the castle, which is also inhabited by three female vampires who attempt to seduce him and drink his blood before Dracula stops them.

Jonathan escapes, and Dracula travels to London on a ship called the *Demeter*. The ship carries fifty boxes of soil that Dracula will use for his coffins as he hunts new victims in England.

Dracula pursues Lucy Westenra, the best friend of Mina Murray, Jonathan's fiancée. Lucy begins sleepwalking at night and grows pale and weak; there are small puncture wounds on her throat one morning. Mina and Lucy's fiancée, Arthur Holmwood, are worried but cannot help her.

Dr. Seward, the administrator of an asylum, is a former suitor of Lucy's. One of his patients is a man named Renfield, who consumes insects and birds in his cell. Renfield is secretly in league with Dracula. When Seward hears of her case he summons his mentor, Abraham Van Helsing. Van Helsing deduces that a vampire is preying on Lucy, but does not tell anyone until he is sure. By then it is too late. Lucy dies of blood loss after several transfusions spread across several days. After Lucy's death, Van Helsing takes Holmwood, Dr. Seward, and Harker to Lucy's tomb. Holmwood pounds a stake through her heart after seeing her, revived, carrying an abducted child.

After Lucy's is killed, Dracula turns his attention to Mina. He forces her to drink his blood and threatens to kill Jonathan. This links Mina to Dracula. The men locate the boxes of earth Dracula uses for shelter and cover them with communion wafers. Dracula transports himself and the final box back to the Carpathians on a ship called the Czarina Catherine. The men find him by using Mina as a sort of tracking device. Her link with Dracula gives them clues to his location. Ultimately, they find Dracula before sunset and Van Helsing kills him. Morris dies during the attack.

Chapters 1-4

Chapter 1 Summary

The book comprises the journal entries, letters, and telegrams written by its characters. Jonathan Harker recounts his trip to Castle Dracula in his journal. He stays at the Golden Kronte Hotel in the village of Bistritz. That night he receives a letter from Dracula welcoming him to the Carpathians.

The next morning, Harker asks the landlord and his wife if they know anything about Dracula. They refuse to answer, but before he leaves, the landlord's wife begs him to stay. She warns him that it is the eve of St. George's Day, and at midnight, "All the evil things in the world will have full sway" (5). When he refuses, she gives him a crucifix.

Before he leaves on the coach, he sees people talking about him. He translates their words with a dictionary: *vampire*, *Satan*, and *hell*. They make the sign of the cross and point at him, their charm against the evil eye. The passengers on the coach look at him with pity and give him gifts, more objects that will protect him from evil.

At the Borgo Pass, Harker switches to a smaller carriage and he and the driver carry on alone. As they travel, dogs and wolves begin to howl, spooking the horses. Harker has the sense that the land is repeating itself over and over and that they are not making progress. They begin to see blue flames. Each time, the driver dismounts and places stones around the flames. At one point wolves encircle them, but the driver commands them to leave and they obey. By the time they reach the castle, Harker is terrified.

Chapter 2 Summary

Harker meets Dracula, who is tall, old, strong, and wears a white mustache. When they shake hands, Harker notices that Dracula has an unnaturally powerful grip and also that his hand is cold. He serves Harker dinner but does not eat. During the dinner, Harker notices other odd features about Dracula: His teeth are sharp, and his ears end in points. There are hairs in the palms of his hands.

The next day Dracula leaves Harker alone. Harker explores his living quarters, the room next to his, and the library. He notices that there are no mirrors anywhere. When Dracula returns they talk in the library. Dracula is interested in mastering the English dialect and diction. He says he learned English from books. Before bed, Dracula says Harker can go anywhere he wishes except rooms that are locked. He abruptly ends their conversation near sunrise.

The next morning, Harker cuts himself shaving when Dracula surprises him by approaching from behind. Harker notices that Dracula has no reflection. When Dracula sees the blood, he reaches for Harker's throat but the crucifix that the landlord's wife gave Harker stops him. Dracula throws the shaving mirror out of the window. After breakfast, Harker explores the castle and realizes he is locked in. Count Dracula is keeping him prisoner.

Chapter 3 Summary

That night Harker and Dracula discuss Transylvania's history. As Dracula answers his questions, he is obviously proud of his heritage. He describes his people as warlike and uncomfortable in the absence of conflict.

During the coming days, the Count quizzes Harker on legal matters. He wants to know how many solicitors he can have. It is obvious that he doesn't want any one person to know too much of his affairs. He instructs Harker to write to whomever he needs that he will stay for a month. He also hopes that Harker only speaks of business in his letters.

Before leaving, Dracula tells Harker not to fall asleep anywhere else in the castle. Once he believes he is alone, Harker hangs the crucifix over his bed and explores the castle further. Later, he looks out the window and sees Dracula crawling down the face of the castle wall. He will see this happen again days later. Then he explores more and tries many locked doors before finding one that he can open.

He falls asleep in this new room. When he wakes, three beautiful young women are there. They talk about kissing him. One of them puts her teeth and lips on his neck. Dracula appears. He reminds them that he warned them not to touch Harker, but they can have Harker when Dracula is through with him. Dracula gives them a bag containing a child to tide them over until they can take control of Harker.

Chapter 4 Summary

Harker wakes in his bed, relieved to be free of the "awful women who were—who *are*—waiting to suck my blood" (42) He goes back to the room where it happened but it is locked. He does not believe that the women were a dream.

On May 19, Dracula asks him to write three letters to Mina and his employer. He wants Harker to put three different dates on them: June 12, June 19, and June 29. Each letter must contain the message that Harker has left the castle and is en route to his home. Harker interprets the date of June 29 as how long he has left to live.

A group of gypsies visit the castle and stay in the courtyard. Harker wants them to help him escape and hopes to pass a letter for Mina to them. However, that night Dracula shows Harker the letter that he handed to one of the gypsies. He burns the letter and says that Harker's trickery is an insult to their friendship.

Days later, he sees Dracula climb out the window, wearing Harker's traveling suit. Harker worries that Dracula is going to impersonate him for some inexplicable reason. Then he hears a woman crying outside. She screams for someone to return her child. Dracula summons a pack of wolves which kill the woman.

Assuming that Dracula is asleep during the day, Harker climbs one of the walls during the daytime and enters Dracula's room. The room is empty. Harker explores and finds a chapel containing the fifty boxes filled with earth. Dracula is asleep on one of them, eyes open.

The next day, Dracula agrees to let Harker leave, but several wolves wait at the door, keeping him inside. He overhears Dracula telling the three women that they can have him the following day.

The next day, Harker returns to the chapel. Dracula is again in the coffin, and younger than Harker has ever seen him. His lips are bloody. Harker realizes he is being used to move Dracula to London so that he can find new victims. He tries to kill the count with a shovel, but Dracula's stare deflects the blade.

Harker hears the gypsies outside and vows to escape or die trying. He takes some of the gold from Dracula's room and begins climbing down the wall.

Chapters 1-4 Analysis

The first four chapters introduce the reader to many of the conventions of a gothic novel. It is worth considering that at *Dracula's* publication in 1897, the vampire legend was not as common as it is now. There were no movie treatments or television programs, and blockbusters like *Twilight* or HBO's *True Blood* had not made vampires a lucrative industry with mass appeal. Reading *Dracula* for the first time in the 19th century, readers would not have anticipated many of the story's events and tropes, even though they may be familiar—even cliché—to a modern audience.

The epistolary nature of the novel helps Stoker maintain suspense throughout the story. The entire book purports to be a record of something that has already occurred. Therefore, the reader does not know if all—or any—of the contributing writers survive.

Harker represents the typical English man of the times. He finds his journey, Dracula, and the castle so disorienting because they are the opposite of Victorian England. His reactions to his experiences—particularly his continuous worry that the unnatural events might be dreams—are similar to those of other characters later in the novel.

The scene with the three vampire women is the best example of this and is also the most overtly sexual scene in the novel. It does a great deal of work portraying Victorian attitudes towards female sexuality. One of the girls kneels before him and then bends over him, an unmistakable suggestion of fellatio. Harker describes her body's movement as "thrilling and repulsive" (39) and here we find the first of the book's descriptions of sexual women as voluptuous. They have "voluptuous lips" (39) and move with a "deliberate voluptuousness" (39). This word reappears later in several of Lucy's final scenes. Harker is horrified, but also wants them to kiss him. The monsters are vampires, but sexually free or aggressive women were also objects of fear and condemnation in Harker's society.

Characters in *Dracula* tend to assume they are dreaming when faced with unnatural, unscientific, irrational events. Harker's delirious state after his encounter with the women introduces the theme of the tenuous line between dreams, memories, and sanity. If the women are real, then Harker is in a deadly, dangerous situation. He is trapped in a castle with monsters that want to drain his blood, which will kill him and turn him into one of them—although he does not know this yet. If he is dreaming or hallucinating, then he still finds himself in a dangerous plight: His mind is betraying him through a sexual fantasy arising from his own subconscious.

The women have power over Harker because they are part of a system—Dracula's castle and the vampiric hierarchy—that is the opposite of the patriarchal Victorian norms. The difference will become clearer in the following chapters, as the reader meets Mina and Lucy.

Chapters 5-9

Chapter 5 Summary

Chapter 5 switches from Harker's journals and pivots to letters written between Mina Murray and her best friend,

Lucy Westenra. There are also journal entries from Mina and Dr. John Seward.

The majority of the communications between Lucy and Mina focus on their romantic prospects. For Mina, this means Jonathan Harker, her fiancé. Lucy has more prospects, having recently received three marriage proposals. Her three suitors are Dr. John Seward, the head of a lunatic asylum, Quiney Morris, a rich American from Texas, and Arthur Holmwood, the English aristocrat, whom she has agreed to marry.

Seward records a diary entry, dictating through a phonograph. He introduces the reader to a patient he is studying: R.M. Renfield, age fifty-nine. Seward distracts himself from Lucy's rejection by focusing on Renfield, who has fascinating delusions.

Chapter 5 concludes with a brief letter from Quincey Morris to Arthur Holmwood, congratulating Arthur on winning Lucy's heart.

Chapter 6 Summary

Mina recounts her visit to the town of Whitby. Lucy takes her to a cliff by the seashore where they talk to Mr. Swales, a longtime resident of Whitby who disdains superstitions and legends. He also tells them that there are many empty graves in the Whitby cemetery because so many of the sailors memorialized there were lost at sea. When he leaves, Lucy tells Mina the plans for her wedding, and Mina confides her fears about Jonathan, whom she has not heard from in a month.

Dr. Seward gives another report on Renfield, whom he classified as a zoophagous (life-eating) maniac. Renfield loves animals, although this is not obvious from his treatment of them. He has the habit of trapping flies with sugar as bait and then using the flies to lure spiders. After catching the spiders, he uses them as bait for sparrows. Renfield sees him eating a blowfly, and later an orderly reports that he ate a bird and spit the bloody feathers out. Renfield claims that the animals make him strong and vital. Then he asks for a cat, claiming that it is the key to his salvation.

Mina writes about her continued worry for Jonathan. She also describes Lucy's troubling new habit of sleepwalking. During a walk, she encounters Mr. Swales again. He suspects that his death is near, but he is not afraid. They see a ship drifting haphazardly by the coast. It appears that no one is steering it.

Chapter 7 Summary

Chapter 7 begins with two newspaper stories about the ship the *Demeter*. During a storm the ship washes ashore. Its crew is missing. The *Demeter's* captain is lashed to the wheel holding a crucifix. When the ship stops at the shore, a massive dog bolts from below decks and escapes. There is nothing on the ship except for dozens of large wooden boxes.

The captain's log describes the *Demeter's* terrible voyage. The story begins with unease among the crew, because a crewman vanishes ten days into the voyage. Another man tells the captain that he saw a tall stranger onboard. They search the ship but find nothing. Men begin disappearing regularly, and soon there are only four left. An inexplicable fog arises and surrounds the ship, making it impossible to approach the harbor. When only the captain and first mate are left, the first mate throws himself into the sea. The captain lashes himself to the wheel.

Mina writes a new entry about Lucy's continued sleepwalking. She and Lucy attend the captain's funeral. Lucy is agitated but it is unclear why. Mina suspects that it might be the death of Mr. Swales bothering her; he was found dead on the cliff with a broken neck and a terrified expression on his face.

Chapter 8 Summary

Mina wakes in the night and sees that Lucy's bed is empty. Mina finds her outside on a bench in the churchyard where they usually sit. When she gets closer, Mina sees a figure with a pale face and red eyes leaning over Lucy, but when she reaches her Lucy is alone. Lucy is short of breath. After she gets Lucy home, Mina notices two small, pinprick-like wounds on Lucy's neck.

Lucy tries to sleepwalk the next two nights, but Mina locks the door to keep her safe. One evening, they go for a walk at sunset. While passing a graveyard, they see a figure near a tombstone. Lucy notices that the sunset has tinged the figure's eyes red.

That night, Lucy sits up in bed, asleep, and points at the window. A large bat circles outside, fluttering its wings against the glass. Lucy grows pale, weak, and sickly over the next few days, and the wounds on her throat grow larger.

A brief piece of legal correspondence follows, providing an invoice for fifty boxes of earth to be delivered to Dracula's house.

Mina's final journal entry of the chapter contains two pieces of news: Lucy's health is improving, and Jonathan has surfaced in a hospital in Budapest, delirious with brain fever.

Chapter 8 concludes with another report from Dr. Seward. Renfield has grown aggressive and arrogant. He tells Seward, "The Master is at hand" (105). Renfield escapes that might and goes to a mansion in Carfax. Seward and several orderlies find him against the door, calling out for his master. They return him to his cell. Straitjacketed and subdued, Renfield begs his master for patience.

Chapter 9 Summary

Mina recounts her journey to Jonathan. Jonathan is now "a wreck of himself" (109) and does not remember the past few weeks. Jonathan gives her his notebook, and asks her to keep and hide it. He says she can read it if she feels the need, but he doesn't want to know what is in it.

A chaplain comes to his bedside and marries them. She seals the book with blue ribbon and wax. It will be their symbol of trust. Lucy writes that she is no longer walking in her sleep and congratulates Mina on her marriage.

Seward provides an update on Renfield: He grows violent during the day but serene at night. In a reversal, he refuses offers of a cat, saying he has more important matters now. He escapes again during an inspection of his room. They find him by the chapel again. His agitation fades and he grows calm when he sees a bat in the sky.

Lucy records her bad dreams in a diary. One night she tries to stay awake but fails. In the morning her throat hurts. She struggles to breathe and recalls that, in her dream, something scraped at her window at night. Seward examines Lucy, but realizes that her condition is beyond his expertise. He asks his teacher, Van Helsing, to examine Lucy and give his opinion.

Seward describes Van Helsing's visit with Lucy. Van Helsing said it was a life and death situation. He charmed her and said she looked wonderful. He also said that she was missing blood, although she was not anemic. Van Helsing refuses to say more, except that he must think.

Renfield briefly resumes capturing flies. But when Seward visits him, he throws the flies out, saying that he is finished with them.

Seward telegrams Van Helsing three times. The first two telegrams report on Lucy's improvement. The third begs him to become because she her condition has worsened terribly.

Chapters 5-9 Analysis

These chapters introduce Mina and Lucy, quickly setting them up as representative stereotypes of idealized Victorian women: virtuous, innocent, young, and good. They stand in total opposition to the lusty vampire women whom Dracula has seduced and corrupted.

One of Lucy's early letters shows that she is the more sexual of the two women. She writes, "Why can't they let a girl marry three men, or as many as want her, and save all this trouble?" (61). Men want her, but she is also capable of desire. It is this expression of her sexual desire that foreshadows Dracula's eventual influence over her.

Their letters also contrast the sunlit, modern life in England with the darkness of Eastern Europe. Whereas the first four chapters of the novel are claustrophobic, frightening, and filled with unnatural acts, like Dracula climbing down the wall of the castle like an animal, in Lucy's and Mina's letters—and in the phonograph entries of Dr. Seward—Western society is depicted as bright, fashionable, and advanced affair.

The letters between Mina and Lucy introduce the other major characters in the novel: Seward, Morris, and Holmwood. Seward is a studious, dedicated scientist who will also serve as the voice of rationality when Van Helsing begins espousing his theories. Morris is a wealthy Texan whose cartoonish slang shows Stoker's poking fun at America's relative lack of sophistication. Holmwood is a noble aristocrat with few distinctive features other than his title. However, the men will overcome the awkwardness of having competed for Lucy's affection and form a team to fight Dracula. They, like Mina and Lucy, are purely good. In a novel that depicts a literal battle against good and evil, they serve as archetypes of righteousness.

Renfield allows Stoker to muse about the relationship between humans and animals. His proclivity for eating small creatures to absorb their power is a scaled-down version of Dracula's consumption of humans. Renfield destroys the spiders and flies, but they fortify him as well. Dracula's victims become, as he will put it to Mina later, "flesh of my flesh; blood of my blood" (303). The relationship between consumption, men, and beasts was particularly relevant to Victorian England at that time. Darwin's pivotal books on evolution had been published in the previous two decades, questioning long-held ideas about creationism. His theories made the boundaries between humans and animals more permeable, suggesting

that there are fewer differences between the two than had
previously been supposed.

Chapters 10-15

Chapter 10 Summary

Lucy's health worries Seward and Holmwood. Shortly after
arriving, Van Helsing gives her a transfusion of
Holmwood's blood. After noticing the puncture wounds on
her neck, Van Helsing asks Seward to stay with Lucy all
night as she sleeps. The night passes uneventfully and Lucy
feels better in the morning.

The next night, Seward falls asleep. The following morning
Lucy is worse. Her lips are white and her skin is pale. They
perform another transfusion, this time with Seward's blood.
A package of garlic flowers arrives for Van Helsing. He
places the flowers around Lucy's neck and rubs them on
the curtains and windowsills of her room.

Chapter 11 Summary

Van Helsing and Seward return to Lucy's home, where her
mother says that she took down the garlic flowers during
the night. When they are alone, Van Helsing is distraught.
Lucy is nearly dead from blood loss. This time, Van
Helsing provides the blood for the transfusion. Afterwards,
Van Helsing tells Lucy's mother that she can't touch
anything he puts in Lucy's room. Four days pass, and Lucy
improves.

An article from the Pall Mall Gazette tells the story of a
wolf that escaped from a zoo. Inexplicably, the wolf
returned the morning after its escape. When it returned, it
was covered in flecks and shards of broken glass.

Renfield surprises Seward by escaping from his cell and rushing into Seward's study with a knife. He cuts Seward's wrist and then falls down as orderlies subdue him. On the floor, he licks the blood, saying, "The blood is the life!" (148).

Van Helsing sends a telegram telling Seward to be at Hillingham that night, but the telegram arrives twenty-two hours late. Lucy wakes in her bed on the night the wolf escaped. She hears howling from the grounds and the flapping noise is at her window again. Her mother enters the room just as a wolf's head bursts through the glass. Lucy faints and her mother slumps over her on the bed.

Four servants enter and see that Mrs. Westenra is dead and Lucy is unconscious. They drink a glass of wine to calm their nerves, but the wine has been drugged and they also lose consciousness. Lucy wakes, and then hides the journal entry in which this event is recorded in the breast of her nightgown, hoping that whoever finds her will be able to find it and learn the truth about that night.

Chapter 12 Summary

Seward writes that he and Van Helsing go to Hillingham. They find the unconscious maids, the body of Mrs. Westenra, and Lucy who is almost dead. The punctures on her neck are larger than before. Morris arrives and offers to give his blood for the transfusion, because Van Helsing and Seward cannot undergo another donation so soon. Holmwood joins them and his presence helps Lucy feel better.

Mina writes to Lucy to tell her about her wedding with Jonathan. She also tells her that Mr. Hawkins invited her and Jonathan to live with him.

Dr. Seward has an assistant named Hennessey. Hennessey writes that Renfield saw two men transporting boxes of earth. He escaped and attacked them before being subdued.

That night as Lucy sleeps, Seward notices that her teeth look sharp. A bat flaps at the window. Lucy is asleep, but she removes the garlic from her throat. When she wakes she pulls the garlic back to her. When Van Helsing arrives, he lifts the handkerchief from her throat. The wounds are gone. He says she is dying and to bring Holmwood.

Holmwood comes into the room and holds her hand. Lucy closes her eyes and her teeth grow longer. She opens her eyes and speaks in a different voice, begging Holmwood to kiss her. Van Helsing, sensing danger, drags him away and forbids him from kissing her. After Lucy dies, Van Helsing allows him to kiss her forehead.

Chapter 13 Summary

Seward describes Van Helsing putting a crucifix in Lucy's mouth and placing garlic in her coffin. He tells Seward that they have to cut Lucy's head off and remove her heart. Seward doesn't understand. The next day, someone steals the crucifix from Lucy's coffin, delaying Van Helsing's plan. Van Helsing asks a grieving Holmwood if he can look through Lucy's papers for clues.

Mina writes that she and Harker were out for a walk when he saw a man he believes is Count Dracula. His shock is so great that he goes to sleep. When he wakes, he has no memory of the episode. Mina decides to read his journal.

That night Mina learns of Lucy's death via telegram. A newspaper article follows the telegram. The story reports on several child abductions, all taking place near Lucy's tomb. The children describe their captor as a "Bloofer Lady" (185). Each child has small puncture wounds on its neck.

Chapter 14 Summary

Mina reads and transcribes Harker's journal. When she meets with Van Helsing, she gives him the diary, understanding that it may help him understand Lucy's death. Van Helsing reads the diary that night and returns it to them the next morning. He believes every word. His confidence helps Harker retrieve his memories of Castle Dracula. He now believes that Dracula is in England, and he begins a new journal.

Seward writes that Renfield is catching flies again. Van Helsing visits and shows Seward the article about the Bloofer Lady; he points out the pinpricks in the children's throats. Seward doubts that there is a connection between Lucy and the article, but Van Helsing urges him to be open-minded and to "believe in things…that you cannot" (202). Van Helsing believes that Lucy is responsible for the punctures on the necks of the abducted children.

Chapter 15 Summary

Seward worries that Van Helsing is insane, but he respects him and agrees to help him with his investigation. They visit one of the abducted children in a hospital and examine his neck. The child's wounds are identical to those on Lucy's neck.

That night, they visit Lucy's tomb and open her coffin. It is empty. They hide outside in the churchyard and wait. Near dawn, Seward notices a white figure. It vanishes when they draw near, but they find that it dropped a child. The child has no marks on its throat. They were just in time. They take it to Hampstead Heath and leave it when they hear a policeman approaching.

They return to Lucy's tomb the next day. They open the coffin and Lucy is there. She is beautiful again. Van Helsing pulls back her lips to show Seward the sharp teeth. He says that he will not kill her yet. Seward begins to believe Van Helsing, who repeats that they must cut off her head and drive a stake through her heart. They explain their plan to Holmwood and Morris. Holmwood is opposed to the desecration of Lucy's body, but agrees to come to the graveyard with Van Helsing.

Chapter 10-15 Analysis

Chapters 10 and 11 introduce the struggle between modern, Western science and older, more traditional forms of truth. Seward evaluates Lucy according to the methods of his profession, but he is unable to explain her blood loss. When Van Helsing begins his investigation in earnest, Stoker shows the reader the value of open-minded inquiry and the limits of medical knowledge. Even the most revered physician would not know to place garlic around Lucy, unless he were open to folklore as a source of truth in the absence of empirical evidence. Ironically, if the Victorians were less rigid, they would be less susceptible to Dracula's threats. Dracula knows that he can move freely under the noses of people who would never accept his potential existence.

The mingling of blood that takes place during the many transfusions gives Stoker another chance to emphasize Lucy's purity. The men who donate their blood to her are as upstanding and righteous as she is, therefore, there is no danger in corrupting her blood with theirs. Van Helsing cannot resist giving the blood moral dimensions, calling it "so pure that we need not defibrinate it" (129). He also refers to Arthur as Lucy's lover throughout the transfusion, giving the process sexual connotations.

Lucy's corruption and death can only be postponed, not stopped. But first, she shows that Dracula's seduction has made her sexually aggressive, not merely a fledgling vampire. When she begs Arthur to kiss her, she sounds ravenous. Van Helsing stops her from endangering Holmwood's body but also his sexual purity. He also shows that Victorian idealism and forbearance can triumph over pure lust.

Stoker emphasizes Lucy's physical beauty after she dies, a sure sign that she is now part of an evil realm. Soon she is abducting children as the Bloofer lady, which is slang for a beautiful woman. Prior to Dracula's seduction of Lucy, Van Helsing would have described her as he does Mina: "[O]ne of God's women, fashioned by His own hand to show us men and other women that there is a heaven where we can enter, and that its light can be here on earth. So true, so sweet, so noble, so little an egoist—and that, let me tell you, is much in this age, so skeptical and selfish" (187). What is the difference between them? Only that Lucy is less prim and more expressive of sexual desire.

Van Helsing will later remind everyone that Dracula cannot enter a residence unless someone invites him in. He destroys Lucy, but Stoker implies that he only does so with her consent. It can be argued that, in the context of the novel and the era, Lucy gives in to lust and pays the price. Chapter 15 shows the depths to which Lucy has descended. There is nothing left of her goodness or humanity. She preys on children and lures them with her beauty, a callback to the child consumed by the women at Castle Dracula.

Chapters 16-21

Chapter 16 Summary

They go to Lucy's tomb, where Van Helsing asks Seward to confirm that Lucy's body was in the coffin the previous day. They open the coffin, find it empty, then go outside and wait. Van Helsing crumbles a communion wafer and wipes the crumbs into the crevices of the door. Lucy appears in a white dress, carrying a child. She bites the child's throat.

The men approach and she drops the child. She begs Arthur to come to her. Her beauty and her inviting aggressiveness tempt the men, but her shameless sexuality repulses them as well. Van Helsing fends her off with a crucifix. He removes the crumbs from the door and Lucy goes into the tomb.

They return the following night. Holmwood kills Lucy by pounding a stake through her heart. He thanks Van Helsing for saving her soul. They agree to meet two nights later to discuss the plan to find and kill Dracula.

Chapter 17 Summary

Jonathan and Mina stay with Seward at the asylum, where Mina transcribes his diary. Seward reads Mina's and Jonathan's diaries as well. He realizes that Dracula is probably staying in the house next to the asylum. Renfield is calm for the moment, and Seward wonders what that could mean about Dracula.

Jonathan investigates the shipping of the boxes. They arrived at the Carfax chapel, but some may have been moved since then. Mina notices that their mission has filled Jonathan with purpose and energy. Holmwood and Morris come to the asylum, where Mina comforts the grieving widower.

Chapter 18 Summary

Mina asks Dr. Seward for permission to visit Renfield. Before she arrives, he eats all of his spiders and flies but behaves politely during her visit. Van Helsing visits the asylum and approves of Mina's transcription and ordering of Seward's diary. He also says that he will not allow her to help them further, because destroying a vampire has "no part for a woman. Even if she be not harmed, her heart may fail her in so much and so many horrors; and hereafter she may suffer" (247).

He tells them the legend of Nosferatu, and lists all of a vampire's strengths and weaknesses. Their success depends on finding the fifty boxes of earth. He repeats that Mina will not take part in their plan but will better serve them by being a symbol of hope.

Chapter 19 Summary

Armed with blessed talismans, the men go to Carfax. The chapel holds twenty-nine boxes; twenty-one are unaccounted for. Rats flood into the room, but the men scare them away by blowing a dog whistle.

Back at the asylum, Van Helsing tries to interrogate Renfield for clues, but the patient won't help him. He insults and curses Van Helsing.

Mina grows more anxious at the asylum. After hearing noises from Renfield's room, she notices that her window is open. Outside, a line of mist creeps across the grounds towards her. She closes the window and goes to sleep but is restless. A white face leans over her, but she thinks she is dreaming.

Chapter 20 Summary

Jonathan learns the location of twelve of the missing boxes. They reside at two separate London houses. The final nine boxes are in Piccadilly. Piccadilly is a busy area; they're unsure of how to get into the house without being seen.

Seward continues to observe Renfield. The patient shows no interest in his insects but repeats that all he wants is life. Seward asks him how he views the fates of the lives he takes. Renfield refuses to talk about souls. Seward believes that Renfield feels guilty about the lives he has consumed, and worries that he might pay a price for them. The next night, attendants find Renfield in a pool of blood.

Chapter 21 Summary

As he dies, Renfield describes his visits from Count Dracula. He says that Dracula made a bargain with him: He would bring Renfield insects and animals to make him strong if Renfield would help with his plans. During Mina's visit, Renfield saw signs (for example, her pale skin) that Dracula had been draining her blood. That night when Dracula visited him, Renfield challenged him. Dracula threw him against the wall and left.

Upstairs, they find Harker in his room, unconscious. Mina is drinking blood from a gash on Dracula's torso. Van Helsing expels Dracula with the host, and Dracula escapes by turning into mist and flowing beneath the door. Then he turns into a bat and flies away. The men find Seward's study destroyed: Dracula tried to destroy all documents pertaining to him. He did not know that they had made copies and hid them in a safe.

Mina and Jonathan wake up. She tells the men that Dracula drank from her throat. He said he would kill Jonathan unless she tasted his blood. It was also not the first time he drained her. He told her that he would make her "flesh of my flesh; blood of my blood; kin of my kin" (303).

Chapters 16-21 Analysis

Lucy's death and Dracula's defilement of Mina are the two pivotal, thematically rich scenes of these chapters.

When the men confront Lucy at the tomb, Stoker focuses on the sexuality of her appearance and words. What was once her purity has transformed into "voluptuous wantonness" (222). When she reaches for Holmwood, Lucy says that her arms are "hungry" (222) for him.

Her words and actions confound the men. They want to indulge her and destroy her in equal measure. She is a temptation, but like all temptations in Victorian society, she has to be destroyed. Similar to Arthur Dimmesdale in *The Scarlet Letter,* the men view their own lust with disdain and guilt. The severity of their revulsion is most evident in Seward's description: "The remnant of my love passed into hate and loathing: had she then to be killed, I could have done it with savage delight" (222). Not only could he kill her in that moment, but he could also rejoice in doing so.

When Holmwood kills Lucy with the stake, Stoker describes him as "driving deeper and deeper" (227) into her. Her body trembles and writhes under the blows, and her gasps and moans give the scene an unmistakably sexual aspect. Stoker uses Holmwood as the executioner because her was her fiancée. Because Lucy and Holmwood were engaged, Holmwood would have allowed her to indulge her sexual desires within their marriage. Because they are never to consummate the act as man and wife, they do so with another form of penetration, one that restores her natural beauty, frees her from carnal evils, and sends her soul to God.

After Lucy dies, Mina is Dracula's next target. The scene where she drinks from the wound on Dracula's chest— almost like a nursing infant—has been a subject of great debate. A nursing child draws life from its mother's breast. Mina draws blood—and her own potential death—from Dracula's. This is the only depiction in the novel of someone feeding on Dracula. He threatens her with Jonathan's death if she resists, but she chooses to participate in her own corruption, mingling Dracula's blood with hers, even though Jonathan would not have wanted her to save his life at the risk of her soul.

Stoker shows Dracula as a disruptor of norms. The scene on the bed is pure ideological disorder with respect to Victorian ideals: Mina is feeding on Dracula while Jonathan, her would-be protector and husband lies helpless and unconscious on the bed with them. As Dracula taunts Mina, he also derides the accepted conventions of the society in which she lives.

Once again, the group banishes the Count with traditional Christian symbols, putting an end to the depravity on the bed. One can argue that Stoker's solution to the moral and societal questions posed in the novel is a regression towards an ever-greater simplicity. Marriage between a man and a woman, with both remaining virgins until their wedding night, is simpler and more sacred than promiscuity and temptation. Christianity is simple in its purity. Its symbols are unchanging, as is their power over evil.

Chapters 22-27

Chapter 22 Summary

Harker writes that Dracula returned to the asylum and broke Renfield's neck. They go to Carfax a day later and sabotage the boxes of earth by placing communion wafers in each one. Before moving on to Piccadilly, Van Helsing fortifies Mina's room with more wafers. He tries to bless her by placing a wafer against her forehead, but it burns her skin. She cries, calling herself unclean.

Chapter 23 Summary

After getting keys to Dracula's other houses, Holmwood and Morris go to the London House. Harker and Van Helsing go to Piccadilly. However, they find only eight boxes there. Dracula has managed to save one. Mina relays a message: Dracula is no longer in Carfax. They wait for him at Piccadilly, certain that they will surprise him. He is weak when he arrives, since the sun is up. He escapes from them by jumping out of a window.

Van Helsing is confident. He places Mina under hypnosis, hoping that she can locate Dracula from a trance state. She hears the sea, and they wonder if this means he is escaping to England by water. Jonathan worries that if he escapes, Mina will eventually turn into a vampire.

Chapter 24 Summary

The men learn that Dracula is on a ship called the Czarina Catherine. It is returning to Varna, the port where Dracula set sail for England after leaving Jonathan. Van Helsing rallies them with a speech about fighting on behalf of all humankind. They will try to catch Dracula in Varna. Mina insists on going with them because she might be able to exploit her link with Dracula to find him.

Chapter 25 Summary

Mina demands that they agree to kill her if she becomes a vampire. They agree and leave for Varna on October 12. Van Helsing believes they will be able to board Dracula's ship when it arrives.

Mina weakens. Then spend one week in Varna before learning that Dracula's ship did not stop there. It waits in Galatz. Van Helsing worries that Dracula's connection to Mina alerted him and helped him learn their plan. He hopes that Dracula is now overconfident and will believe they have given up.

Chapter 26 Summary

Mina's trances reveal fewer details. However, she hears the sound of water. They believe he is still near the water. When they reach Galatz they learn that the box was taken by a trader named Petrof Skinsky. Skinsky's body is found in a graveyard with his throat torn out.

Mina gives them various routes that he could have taken. They divide forces and cover the routes. Jonathan and Arthur take a steamboat while Mina and Van Helsing go to Castle Dracula. Seward and Morris take horses. At the town of Veresti, Mina and Van Helsing take a carriage, traversing the same route Jonathan did.

Chapter 27 Summary

En route to the castle, Van Helsing learns that he can no longer hypnotize Mina. After making camp that night, Van Helsing crumbles the communion wafers and draws a protective ring on the ground around her. The three vampires from the castle appear. The horses are so frightened that they die. Van Helsing and Mina resist the vampires' attempts to lure them out of the ring.

Van Helsing goes ahead as Mina sleeps inside the ring of wafers. After reaching the castle, he finds the tomb of the beautiful vampires and destroys them. He finds Dracula's tomb and covers it in wafers. He also seals the castle door. They leave the castle and head towards the others. Wolves howl around them during a snowstorm. They see gypsies pulling a cart with a box of earth. Seward, Jonathan, Arthur, and Morris storm the cart and fight the gypsies. They throw the cart to the ground. Morris is wounded. Arthur and Seward aim their rifles at the gypsies.

Harker cuts Dracula's throat. Morris stabs him in the heart with a knife. Dracula turns to dust. He looks peaceful, which surprises Mina. Morris dies.

Seven years later, a coda reveals that the Harkers have a son named Quincey. Seward and Arthur are both happily married. Van Helsing says that one day their son will know how much they loved Mina, and how much they risked for her.

Chapters 22-27 Analysis

The final chapters of the book accelerate in pace, mimicking Dracula's frantic attempt to escape.

Mina gains greater significance to the plot, but remains underdeveloped. Consider Jonathan's description of her after she falls asleep: "Mina is sleeping now, calmly and sweetly like a little child. Her lips are curved and her face beams with happiness. Thank God there are such moments still for her" (343). Stoker does not portray her as having depth or ambitions beyond being a good wife and Christian. She is an infantilized prop and a plot device for the men to observe and protect in service of their own Christian glory.

Dracula knows that his dominion over Mina will give him power of the men who love her. On a macro level, given that the reader knows his plans for expansion, his conquest of Mina would be a prelude to his conquest of all English women. Mina intuits this as well, which is why she insists on her death should she become a vampire.

Driving Dracula out of England is the first major victory for the men. They have never seen the vampire on the defensive. Unfortunately, he remains a formidable opponent while on the run.

The female vampires make one last appearance to tempt Van Helsing and to recruit Mina. Like previous descriptions of them, they have "voluptuous lips" (387). Van Helsing is simultaneously beset with the urge to kill them and to give in to their seduction.

The gypsies protect Dracula because they are part of the old, superstitious world that aligns itself against Christianity. They rush Dracula's coffin to his castle because he is the novel's most potent symbol of Eastern European power. If they can help him survive, they can help prolong their way of life, thinking, and remain in a world with folk magic, instead of making peace with the modern areas of Europe.

The final chapters are the most suspenseful and fast moving. The men literally race against the setting sun to reach Dracula before he can become mobile at sunset. The weather worsens. This is a reminder that the weather in Eastern Europe is harsher than that shown in England in the novel. The Carpathians are all storms and wind, forces that cannot be restrained or controlled. They are natural phenomena that are presented as unnatural in the novel, because the weather in London—other than descriptions of sunny days—in plays little part in the plot. Outside of England the weather almost serves as another character, a malevolent force that aids Dracula.

When Van Helsing kills the female vampires, they are so beautiful in their repose that he grows weak and nearly feels remorse. He hesitates, but knows that when the first one wakes, "The beautiful eyes of the fair woman open and look love, and the voluptuous mouth present to a kiss—and a man is weak. And there remain one more victim in the Vampire fold; one more to swell the grim and grisly ranks of the Un-Dead!" (390). When he opens the coffin of the most beautiful vampire, "She was so fair to look on, so radiantly beautiful, so exquisitely voluptuous, that the very instinct of man in me, which calls some of my sex to love and to protect one of hers, made my head whirl with new emotion" (391). Stoker uses Van Helsing's momentary reluctance to show the consequences of giving in to temptation. If he allowed the seduction, he would become a "victim." A Victorian man whose morals crumble under the weight of lust simply becomes another indulgent, wanton vampire. Van Helsing resists because the "instinct of man" is to protect women, even from their own sexuality. Rather than allow the temptation, he releases the souls of the female vampires by killing them and granting them peace.

When Dracula dies, he is also peaceful. Throughout the novel, he has been confident, driven, cruel, aggressive, and powerful. There has never been any indication that he is not at peace with his situation. But Mina's observation holds greater weight since it is she that most often notices when men are calm—and is often responsible for that calmness: "A look of peace, such as I never could have imagined might have rested there" (397). Dracula can no longer harm anyone, and one can argue that the peace on his face— similar to that of Lucy's face when she died—suggests that even his soul was redeemable.

The novel's brief coda demonstrates that, having taken righteous action, the men all move on with their lives and all is well. Van Helsing suggests that the takeaway of the entire story is that men loved Mina enough to risk their lives for her. Mina represents everything the Victorians considered good and worthwhile: righteousness, chastity, an ability to bolster and embolden men, and the maternal instinct. The modern world has vanquished the old world, and the enlightened West has once again shown itself to be more than a match for the superstitious East.

Count Dracula

Dracula is a vampire who has lived for centuries. He is a proud descendant of the warlike Huns and he misses the days of war. Initially, he presents himself to Jonathan Harker as an erudite, amiable nobleman who prioritizes hospitality and generosity. However, Dracula reveals himself to be a creature of sadistic cruelty and evil appetites. He possesses great strength, the ability to command animals, to shapeshift, and has some influence over the weather. He is weak to garlic, the sign of the cross, the crucifix, daylight, and the communion wafer.

Jonathan Harker

Jonathan Harker is a lawyer who provides the reader's first exposure to Dracula. Jonathan visits Castle Dracula on behalf of his firm, which is brokering a real estate deal with the Count. During his time in the castle, Jonathan is brave, curious, and finally, determined to escape. The shock of his experience weakens him. However, once he learns that his experience was real—and not the result of a brain fever— he is tenacious and bold in his efforts to protect Mina and defeat Dracula.

Mina Murray

When the novel begins, Mina is engaged to Jonathan Harker. She works as a schoolteacher. Mina—particularly when compared to Lucy, her best friend—represents an incorruptible Christianity and purity. She is the ideal Victorian woman: chaste, prim, supportive of her husband and the men in her life, and resourceful. She is also clever and practical. Her resourcefulness is particularly apparent when she collates the journals into a cohesive narrative. The men rely on her for comfort and sympathy, and it is her presence that often restores them resolute determination. Mina becomes one of Dracula's victims, but when Dracula dies, his hold on her—and the fear that she will eventually become a vampire—dies. Van Helsing will remark at the novel's conclusion that saving Mina—and by proxy, preserving the way of life that she represented—was the entire point of the story.

Lucy Westenra

Lucy is Mina's best friend. Stoker portrays her as more beautiful, flirtatious, and sensual than Mina. In one journal entry Lucy tells Mina of three separate marriage proposals she just received, and wonders why a girl can't indulge herself and marry as many men as she chooses. However, she maintains her chastity until she becomes Dracula's first victim in the novel. After she becomes a vampire, Stoker describes her as ravenous, wanton, and voluptuous. She becomes a creature of pure appetite that preys on children. Her sexualized state tests the men's ability to resist temptation, even after she is a vampire. After her final death, she regains her purity and innocence as her soul is saved. Lucy symbolizes the consequences of giving in to sexual desire outside of Christian marriage.

Doctor John Seward

Dr. Seward was a pupil of Van Helsing. He is in charge of a mental asylum in London. Throughout most of the story, Seward catalogues his interactions with a patient named Renfield. Seward is devoted to Lucy even after she rejects his marriage proposal, and he is present for most of the pivotal events in the book once the main characters are all in London. He skepticism plays a useful counterpoint to

Van Helsing's more expansive metaphysics, and he often serves as a stand in for the rationalist arguments against the supernatural.

Renfield

Renfield is a pitiable, disturbed patient at Dr. Seward's asylum. He spends his time devouring insects and birds. Seward classifies Renfield as a consumer of life seeking greater strength through this consumption. Renfield falls under Dracula's spell and helps him in exchange for what he hopes will be eternal life. Dracula eventually kills him, showing that even though Renfield helped him, Dracula has no real allies.

Abraham Van Helsing

Van Helsing is a learned philosopher, scientist, doctor, and metaphysician. He is also the teacher of Dr. Seward. Van Helsing is more open-minded than the other characters in the novel. He is not a worshipper of western medicine and knows that there are evils that cannot be conquered by reason and dogma. He is a kind, brave man who treats Lucy, Mina, Harker, and the other members of their party as if they were his beloved children. His knowledge of history and folklore make him the perfect antagonist for Dracula, whom he ultimately defeats.

Arthur Holmwood

Shortly after the novel begins, Arthur becomes Lucy's fiancé. He comes from an aristocratic family and becomes Lord Godalming over the course of the story. He is the only other aristocrat in the novel besides Count Dracula. Stoker uses Arthur to show that not every nobleman is as cold, aloof, and avaricious as Dracula. Arthur shows extreme devotion to Lucy in both his grief at her death, and his willingness to save her soul by pounding the stake into her heart. Arthur is brave, loyal to his friends, and willing to do what he considers the right thing, even when it is difficult.

Quincey Morris

Morris is another of Lucy's suitors. He is a wealthy American from the state of Texas. He provides blood for one of Lucy's transfusions, and he is present at her tomb when Holmwood frees her soul. Morris joins the men in their pursuit of Dracula and dies during the gypsy attack prior to Dracula's death. He serves primarily as one of Mina's protectors. He is righteous, good-hearted, brave, and happy to sacrifice his life in order to save Mina.

Christianity as Salvation

The most effective deterrents to evil in *Dracula* are the crucifix and the Host, or communion wafer. Ironically, Van Helsing knows of their potential efficacy because of his study of folklore. Christian canon does not list the Host and the crucifix as weapons against vampires because vampires do not exist in Christian doctrine.

Dracula makes a convenient substitute for the Christian Satan. He is seductive, charming, hedonistic, and his pointed ears and sharp teeth give him the look of a predator. He preys on women and transforms them into dangerously sexual beings. Dracula uses pleasure as a temptation and a weapon.

Dracula may have eternal life, but it is only terrestrial life on earth. His immortality has no bearing on salvation or an afterlife. This is why Arthur is able to kill Lucy with the stake. He does not want her trapped on earth forever as a vampire. By killing her vampire form, he is able to save her soul and usher it to the Christian heaven.

Dracula's stance on Christianity is more open-minded than it might first appear. The symbols of Christianity work as weapons, but there is no requirement that the wielders of the weapons be zealous believers. They all speak of Christian values but not in terms of Jesus Christ as their ultimate savior. They are faithful and nominally Christian, but Stoker gives the impression that anyone who wielded a crucifix against a vampire would succeed, regardless of the degree of their belief. In this way, Christianity in the novel is more of a utilitarian tool against a powerful enemy than an deeply held and personal faith.

The Old World versus the Modern

One of Jonathan's first impressions of Castle Dracula is how old it is. The "old centuries" unsettle him. He describes the castle as having power that cannot be killed by the onset of the modern era. The Victorian era was upended in the late 1800s. England had been a society based on agriculture. The Industrial Revolution threatened farmers, expanded the possibilities of agricultural commerce, and wrought changes in the farmers' lives. In addition, the theories of Charles Darwin and other scientific thinkers threatened the dogmas of Christianity, whose tenets informed most aspects of English life.

Stoker presents the old world as primitive and aggressive. Dracula represents this old world of aggression and hostility. He delivers his monologue about his warlike ancestors with pride and nostalgia. However, the decrepitude of Castle Dracula contrasts starkly with the glamor, polish, and technological sophistication of modern London. When Jonathan sees Dracula in the street, he is young again; even he has been given an upgrade by moving into the modern age.

Van Helsing serves as a bridge between the two ages. He is able to fight Dracula because he embraces all useful knowledge. He studies both eastern and western philosophies and medicine. Like a scientist, he is primarily interested in results—in what works and solves problems. But like a folklorist, anthropologist, and metaphysician, he does not discount the value of anecdotal evidence, ritual, and so-called superstition.

The Danger of Female Sexuality

Women who are sexually aggressive or who give in to seduction are punished and destroyed in *Dracula*. The theme first arises during Jonathan's encounter with the three vampire women in the castle. When they caress and kiss him, they represent pure, unfettered lust. Jonathan describes them as "Devils of the pit!" (55), unlike the pure Mina in every way.

If the battle between Dracula and the men can be framed as a battle between good and evil, it is played on the field of women's sexuality. Lucy and Mina are underdeveloped characters, as was common in Victorian era literature. A sexually free, promiscuous woman would be a disgraced pariah in Victorian society, worthy of shunning. Victorian norms required that a woman be a wife or a virgin. There were no gray areas.

At the beginning of the novel, Lucy and Mina are both young, innocent women, although Lucy's letters betray a more flirtatious temperament than Mina's. Lucy is beset with suitors. She accepts Arthur's marriage proposal, but it is Dracula who seduces and possesses her, a temporary triumph of the old, heathen world over sexuality of a young Christian woman. As soon as she is in Dracula's thrall, Stoker begins describing Lucy's beauty as voluptuous, and any woman described as voluptuous in the novel dies by the end, destroyed by Christian hands. When Dracula gains influence over Mina, the men are threatened, not only for her life and her soul, but also by the fear that she will become promiscuous.

Insanity, Dreams, and Fallibility

Many of the characters in *Dracula* confront events that are literally unbelievable in the moment. They find refuge in attributing their experiences to dreams or insanity. Harker finds himself unable to rely even on his memories. Late in the novel, Seward suspects that they have all gone mad and will wake in straitjackets. Lucy, Mina, Van Helsing, and Harker all experience uncanny events that they believe to be dreams, rather than to accept the unnatural as real.

The characters' rationality—and the misdirection they give themselves by insisting that they are dreaming—works to Dracula's advantage. Every moment they spend wondering if they are dreaming, or mad, is a moment that they are not focusing on the real threat.

Renfield is the novel's most overt symbol of insanity. He is locked in a lunatic asylum, he eats insects, and his babbling rarely seems coherent. Renfield is not as insane as he seems, however. Much of his muttering is actual communication with Dracula, who is using him to achieve his own ends.

Outsiders as the Other

Dracula lives in an isolated castle in an ancient part of the country. While Jonathan travels to visit him, the people pity him because he is an outsider in their lands; he does not know the dangers that await him, because he does not know the legends about vampires.

Dracula is aware that he is different from others. He explains his desire to speak perfect English to Jonathan as necessary: "But a stranger in a strange land, he is no one; men know him not—and to know not is to care not for. I am content if I am like the rest, so that no man stops if he see me, or pause in his speaking if he hear my words, to say, "Ha, ha! a stranger!" (21). He lays out his plans for Jonathan. He does not want to seem like an outsider, because it will limit his ability to move quietly.

Dracula is the only threatening figure in the novel—save for Renfield, whose actions are a function of a ruined mind, not of malice. He is also the only character who is not of English, Dutch, or American heritage. His arrival in London is a literal invasion of England, and his plan to create more vampires is something of an invasion upon the human species as a whole.

One's outsider status depends on context. When Harker travels to Castle Dracula, the peasants he meets along the way treat him as an outsider, even though they wish for his well-being. He feels that he is an outsider who has wandered into a world of superstitious people who believe the evil eye can ward off malevolence. The nomadic gypsies are outsiders everywhere they go, having no permanent homes.

In the larger, global context of the novel, any encroachment by the East upon the West—or vice versa—is an outsider entering unfamiliar terrain. The mistrust of the other can have its foundation in differences of religious, ideology, science, medicine, rationality, magic, and folklore.

Blood

Blood is the essence of life in *Dracula*. For vampires, it is the food that allows them to live forever. For mortals, blood is the substance that keeps their hearts beating, and which makes them prey for Dracula. Blood is often the most obvious sign that violence has been done to someone. Blood also has sexual connotations, given its relationship to intercourse, virginity, and fertility. It is also a corrupting force. When Dracula gains access to Mina's mind, it is because he forces her to drink his blood, mixing it with her own.

Wolves

Wolves appear throughout the novel, beginning with Jonathan's journey to Castle Dracula. Wolves symbolize the predatory nature of the vampires. They are feared in the wild, and are willing to attack people in villages if hunger—and a lack of prey—forces them from the woods. Dracula is able to command the wolves, and can also become a wolf. Every appearance of a wolf is threatening, because wolves are always a danger. They are driven by appetite and are fearless fighters.

The Host and the Crucifix

Van Helsing brings communion wafers—known as The Host—from Amsterdam. The wafers act as barriers to evil, particularly the heathen evil of the vampires. The communion wafers represent the body of Jesus Christ. The presence of Christ—with the wafers serving as his proxy—allows Van Helsing to seal off Lucy's tomb, prevent Dracula from entering his castle, and creating a ring around

Mina that the wolves cannot pass. The crucifix also symbolizes the triumph of Christianity as the ultimate sign of Christian authority. Each time the cross appears, it repels a vampire.

The Three Female Vampires

The three women in the castle symbolize aggressive female sexuality. They are overt in their desires and eager to openly display their appetites. During their initial meeting with Jonathan, he is both titillated and appalled. His interactions with Mina have no sexual tension, and his attraction to her is described only in terms of her goodness and innocence. Stoker wrote *Dracula* during the Victorian era. The three vampire women are the opposite of the faith, modesty, and primness of idealized Victorian women. Their destruction represents the triumph of chasteness and innocence over lascivious appetites.

The Stake

The stake is the weapon that Arthur kills Lucy with. It is an unambiguous phallic symbol, particularly when wielded by Arthur, who was to marry Lucy. A stake has only one purpose: to penetrate. The stake is also a reminder of the consequences of giving in to temptation. Throughout the novel, Stoker reiterates that vampires can only prey on willing victims. Lucy allows Dracula to seduce her. Her death at the point of the stake is her punishment for inviting Dracula—consciously or not—Into her flesh. Stoker describes the act of Lucy's death in sexual terms. Lucy writhes, moans, and quivers during the penetration. When she is dead, she is restored to her former purity, and Van Helsing allows Arthur to kiss her.

The Czarina Catherine

When Dracula attempts to return to his castle, he does so above the ship the Czarina Catherine. Catherine was a Russian noblewoman with legendarily promiscuous appetites. Dracula's use of her namesake to escape from chaste Christian men symbolizes the (ultimately futile) battle that evil and sexual licentiousness wage with Christianity and sexual purity. If Mina were to become a vampire, the Czarina Catherine represents the sexual depths to which she would fall.

1. "But a stranger in a strange land, he is no one; men know him not—and to know not is to care not for. I am content if I am like the rest, so that no man stops if he see me, or pause in his speaking if he hear my words, to say, "Ha, ha! a stranger!" (Chapter 2, Page 21)

   Dracula foreshadows his plans to move to London and some of his motivations for learning English so well. He wants to be able to blend in, so that no one can mistake him for a stranger. His eventual crimes would cast suspicion on outsiders or newcomers first, and he wants to remove that possibility.

2. "There is a reason why all things are as they are." (Chapter 2, Page 22)

   Dracula tells Jonathan not to try the locked doors in the castle, but his statement foreshadows his ability to plan meticulously. Dracula's move to London requires great resources, coordination, and audacity. He believes in the predestination of his own success, and will model his takeover of London similarly to the control he exerts over his castle.

3. "Despair has its own calms." (Chapter 4, Page 45)

   Jonathan sleeps after the Count tells him to make the letters. He is beginning to accept his fate; he is trapped. He counts on his dreams to find peace. This foreshadows the importance of dreams to other characters, later in the novel. Their dreams are nightmarish, and they often confuse dreams with reality.

4. "I am alone in the castle with those awful women. Faugh! Mina is a woman, and there is nought in common. They are devils of the Pit!" (Chapter 4, Page 55)

Jonathan contrasts Mina with the women at the castle. The major difference as Stoker presents them is that the vampires are lascivious, while Mina is pure. Jonathan thinks of women in terms of their innocence, not of their features. The vampires are not women because they are sexually aggressive and corrupt.

5. "I suppose that we women are such cowards that we think a man will save us from fears, and we marry him. I know now what I would do if I were man and wanted to make a girl love me." (Chapter 5, Page 60)

Lucy writes to Mina about her proposals. She is self-aware, and knows what her motivations for considering marriage are. She sees men as an instrument to reduce fears. Ironically, over the course of the novel it becomes clear that men see themselves that way as well. In Lucy's case, she experiences horrific fear and the men fail to save her from Dracula's advances.

6. "Some of the 'New Women' writers will some day start an idea that men and women should be allowed to see each other asleep before proposing or accepting. But I suppose the New Woman won't condescend in the future to accept; she will do the proposing herself. And a nice job she will make of it, too! There's some consolation in that." (Chapter 8, Page 94)

Mina pokes fun at the progressive feminist writers who would like women to have more agency. She finds the idea of men and women seeing each other asleep before

marriage as laughable as women proposing to men.
The New Woman is not interested in equality between
men and women, as far as Mina can tell. The New
Woman wants to be in charge.

7. "I am here to do Your bidding, Master. I am Your
    slave, and You will reward me, for I shall be faithful."
    (Chapter 8, Page 107)

    Seward hears Renfield muttering in his cell. Renfield's
    words show the depths of control that Dracula gains
    over his victims. His devotion implies that Dracula
    promises rewards to some of the people he manipulates.
    In this case, the reader learns later that Dracula has
    promised Renfield an endless stream of lives to
    consume.

8. "Remember my friend, that knowledge is stronger than
    memory, and we should not trust the weaker." (Chapter
    10, Page 126)

    Van Helsing explains the value of knowledge to
    Seward. Their own memories matter little in their
    struggle against Dracula, who can only be fought with
    knowledge. His statement also refers to the whole of
    scientific and anthropological record. Knowledge is
    preserved through writing, in part, as a bulwark
    against the decay of memory.

9. "We learn from failure, not from success!" (Chapter 10,
    Page 126)

    Van Helsing tells Seward about the value of the
    scientific method. Every breakthrough is built upon
    failed experiments. Failure teaches more lessons than
    success. Failure against Dracula will result in their

deaths, their enslavement in eternity, and possibly the corruption or destruction of the human race. Their fight against Dracula is an experiment that they will not have the chance to repeat.

10. "The blood is the life! The blood is the life!" (Chapter 11, Page 148)

Renfield shouts as he licks up the blood on the floor. Before Seward knows about Renfield's connection to Dracula, he believes the behavior is insane. But blood is what sustains Dracula, and the blood of others is what gives him eternal life. For Renfield, consuming the human blood on the floor is a more potent version of the lives of the animals he consumes.

11. "There are darknesses in life and there are lights, and you are one of the lights, the light of all lights." (Chapter 14, Page 192)

Van Helsing is grateful to Mina for the documents. Her resourcefulness helps them create a plan. The men in the novel typically describe Mina as a source of light, hope, and goodness. Van Helsing calls her the light of all lights, foreshadowing the gravity of Dracula's eventual focus on her. If the light of all lights can be extinguished, no English women are safe.

12. "It is the fault of our science that it wants to explain all; and if it explain not, then it says there is nothing to explain." (Chapter 14, Page 200)

Van Helsing is more open-minded than other doctors and scientists. He knows that science cannot answer all questions. The scientific method promises answers—or at least sound theories—for those who use it. Empirical

evidence is not enough for Van Helsing. To fight
Dracula, he cannot rely on science alone; he needs his
belief in anecdotal evidence and his mastery of folklore.

13. "I want you to believe...to believe in things that you
    cannot." (Chapter 14, Page 202)

    Because he was Seward's teacher, Van Helsing
    understands Seward's innate resistance to irrationality
    and untestable hypotheses. Seward must have faith to
    help Van Helsing—to believe, if only temporarily, in
    something that he cannot prove scientifically. But
    because he chooses to suspend his belief, he is able to
    witness, empirically and unequivocally, Lucy's undead
    status.

14. "There in the coffin lay no longer the foul Thing that
    we had so dreaded and grown to hate that the work of
    her destruction was yielded as a privilege to the one
    best entitled to it, but Lucy as we had seen her in life,
    with her face of unequalled sweetness and purity."
    (Chapter 16, Page 227)

    Stoker emphasizes that Lucy's purity is restored when
    the vampire version of her dies. Her face is sweet and
    bright, not flushed and aroused. Her death restores her
    soul to a peaceful state. Van Helsing will witness the
    same phenomena when he kills the three female
    vampires at the castle, and Mina will make a similar
    observation when Dracula dies.

15. "I suppose there is something in woman's nature that
    makes a man free to break down before her and express
    his feelings on the tender or emotional side without
    feeling it derogatory to his manhood." (Chapter 17,
    Page 241)

Mina lets Arthur sob and knows that her presence comforts him. She does not view herself as a powerful figure, but as someone who can assist a man with his grief. Stoker shows that men need to be able to express their grief, but that they are uncomfortable doing it in each other's presence, because emotional comfort is not one of the men's duties.

16. "We women have something of the mother in us that makes us rise above smaller matters when the mother-spirit is invoked; I felt this big, sorrowing man's head resting on me, as though it were that of the baby that may someday lie on my bosom, and I stroked his hair as though he were my own child." (Chapter 17, Page 242)

It is not only the men who characterize women in the novel as having different attributes than men. Mina sees herself as playing a maternal role and being someone who dispenses with petty troubles when men cannot. Many aspires to motherhood, to being a useful wife, and to helping the men in their quest. Her own needs align with their, which is typical of the Victorian ideal of women.

17. "No one but a woman can help a man when he is in trouble of the heart." (Chapter 17, Page 243)

Quincey Morris sees Mina after she has been comforting Holmwood. When women in the novel are essential, it is only because of the effect they have on men, or as avatars of goodness for men to protect. Mina and Lucy exist only in states of needing protection, offering comfort, or attempting to seduce their victims.

18. "A year ago which of us would have received such a possibility, in the midst of our scientific, matter-of-fact nineteenth century?" (Chapter 18, Page 251)

Science can give one the impression that they already know enough about a subject. The achievement of knowledge can diminish the desire to understand. This attitude leads to less progress. It would also make them less safe. To fight vampires, Van Helsing says that they have nothing except superstition and tradition to learn from.

19. "I am truly thankful that she is to be left out of our future work, and even of our deliberations. It is too great a strain for a woman to bear. I did not think so at first, but I know better know." (Chapter 19, Page 267)

Harker watches Mina sleeping. It is ironic that, even though Mina will play a pivotal role in finding and defeating Dracula, her husband does not think she can be included in their planning. In fact, he admits that his mistake was in giving her too much credit, and viewing her as more resilient than has proven to be the case.

20. "Doctor, as to life, what is it after all? When you've got all you require, and you know that you will never want, that is all." (Chapter 20, Page 284)

This is Renfield's view on life, when he still hopes that Dracula will grant him eternal life. He corrupts the cheery axiom that a man who has everything he needs is already a rich man. Renfield has life, but he does not have the undead, eternal life that he craves. He will never want, because he will have eternity to pursue his desires if Dracula makes him a vampire.

21. "I sometimes think we must be all mad and that we shall wake to sanity in strait-waistcoats." (Chapter 20, Page 289)

Dr. Seward's conversations with Renfield—combined with the fight against Dracula—make Seward question his sanity. He knows that he is abandoning rationality to fight against a being that science dictates should not exist. His confusion is similar to that of the other characters who convince themselves that they are dreaming when they experience something uncanny.

22. "Unclean, unclean! I must touch him or kiss him no more. Oh, that it should be that it is I who am now his worst enemy, and whom he may have most cause to fear." (Chapter 21, Page 300)

After being forced to drink Dracula's blood, Mina's only thought is that she is ruined for Jonathan. She doesn't see her defilement as an act perpetrated against herself but rather against Jonathan and their marriage. She is unclean, traumatized, but speaks as if the greatest wrong has been done to her husband. Once again, a Victorian woman's torment serves as a plot device in a story about heroic Victorian men.

23. "My revenge is just begun! Your girls that you all love are mine already; and though them you and others shall yet be mine—my creatures, to do my bidding and to be my jackals when I want to feed." (Chapter 23, Page 323)

Dracula reveals that he planned on using Lucy and Mina as weapons against the men. If he can corrupt women, he knows that their sexual allure will be irresistible to many men. They can help Dracula

*compound his victims, create more vampires, and
spread across England. This is another example of
women being used as props. In this case, they are bait
for men.*

24. "I want you to bear something in mind though all this
dreadful time...That poor soul who has wrought all this
misery is the saddest case of all. Just think what will be
his joy when he too is destroyed in his worser part that
his better part may have spiritual immortality."
(Chapter 23, Page 325)

*Mina realizes that Dracula must have also been
someone's victim. She reminds the men that, just as
Lucy had no peace while she was driven by pure
appetite, Dracula must feel the same way. He is
powerful but wretched. Christianity insists that sins can
be forgiven and that no souls are beyond salvation.
Despite being one of Dracula's victims, she still views
their pursuit of him as a chance to bring him eternal
peace.*

25. "I shall be glad as long as I live that even in that
moment of final dissolution there was in the face a look
of peace, such as I never could have imagined might
have rested there." (Chapter 27, Page 397)

*Mina describes Dracula's peace in his final moment.
Her instinct that he was a pitiable, tormented creature
prove correct. Killing him is a mercy. When Holmwood
drove the stake through Lucy's heart, she found the
same peace and found salvation, her purity regained.
Dracula's face experiences the same change, and his
spiritual eternity will be better than his immortality on
earth.*

ESSAY TOPICS

1. What is the role of religion in *Dracula*? How does Christianity serve the characters in their fight against Dracula?

2. Discuss the relationship between superstition and reason in the novel.

3. Why did Stoker choose to tell the story in letters, journal entries, and telegrams? Would the story be better served by a more straightforward narrative? Why or why not?

4. What was the enormous dog that escaped from the ship? Why was it never found?

5. What does Van Helsing mean when he tells Seward that he wants him to believe things that he cannot?

6. What is the significance of Lucy's sleepwalking?

7. Discuss the novel's attitudes towards female sexuality.

8. Why does Renfield consume lives? What effect does his case have on the rest of the story?

9. Why do you think that Dracula only seems to choose young and beautiful victims?

10. Why is Van Helsing so much more open-minded than other scientists and doctors?

Made in the USA
Monee, IL
27 February 2022

91958993R00036